W9-AJO-581

WITHDRAWN

South America

by Mike Graf

Consultant:
Catherine H. Helgeland
Professor of Geography
University of Wisconsin–Manitowoc
Manitowoc, Wisconsin

Bridgestone Books
an imprint of Capstone Press
Mankato, Minnesota

Bridgestone Books are published by Capstone Press
151 Good Counsel Drive, P.O. Box 669, Mankato, Minnesota 56002
http://www.capstone-press.com

Copyright © 2003 by Capstone Press. All rights reserved.
No part of this publication may be reproduced in whole or in part, or stored in a retrieval
system, or transmitted in any form or by any means, electronic, mechanical, photocopying,
recording, or otherwise, without written permission of the publisher.
For information regarding permission, write to Capstone Press,
151 Good Counsel Drive, P.O. Box 669, Dept. R, Mankato, Minnesota 56002
Printed in the United States of America.

Library of Congress Cataloging-in-Publication Data
Graf, Mike.
    South America/by Mike Graf.
    p. cm.—(Continents)
    Summary: Describes the regions, landforms, people, and interesting places of the
South American continent.
    ISBN 0-7368-1421-3 (hardcover)
    1. South America—Juvenile literature. 2. South America—Geography—Juvenile
literature. I. Title. II. Continents (Mankato, Minn.)
F2208.5 .G73 2003
918—dc21
                                                    2002000397

Editorial Credits
Erika Mikkelson, editor; Karen Risch, product planning editor; Linda Clavel, designer and
    illustrator; Image Select International, photo researchers

Photo Credits
Andre Jenny/Focus Group/PictureQuest, 21
Art Directors and TRIP/M. Barlow, 11; M. Jeliffe, 13; B. Gadsby, 16, F. Good, 22
    (Lake Titicaca); T. Bognar, 22 (Iguazú Falls)
Digital Wisdom/Mountain High, cover
Eyewire, 17
ImageState, 15, 18
Photodisc, Inc., 19, 22 (Machu Picchu)
Rob Crandall/ Stock Connection/PictureQuest, 20

1 2 3 4 5 6 07 06 05 04 03 02

Table of Contents

Fast Facts about South America

Population: 346 million (early 2000s estimate)

Number of countries: 13

Largest cities: São Paulo, Brazil; Buenos Aires, Argentina; Lima, Peru

Highest point: Mount Aconcagua, 22,834 feet (6,960 meters) tall

Lowest point: Valdés Peninsula, 151 feet (46 meters) below sea level

Longest river: Amazon River, 4,080 miles (6,566 kilometers) long

Size of South America compared to the United States

Amazon River

● Lima

● São Paulo

▲ Mount Aconcagua

● Buenos Aires

Valdés Peninsula ▼

Key
- ● City
- ▲ Highest Point
- ▼ Lowest Point

N
W ● E
S

Countries in South America

1. Ecuador
2. Colombia
3. Venezuela
4. Guyana
5. Suriname
6. French Guiana (belongs to France)
7. Peru
8. Brazil
9. Bolivia
10. Paraguay
11. Chile
12. Uruguay
13. Argentina

South America

South America is the fourth largest continent. The Caribbean Sea lies north of South America. The Atlantic Ocean is to the east. The Pacific Ocean is west of South America. Antarctica lies to the south.

PACIFIC OCEAN

CARIBBEAN SEA

ATLANTIC OCEAN

N

W   E

S

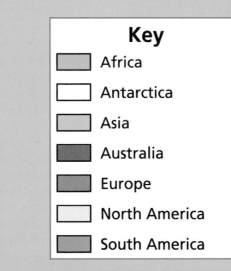

Key

▢	Africa
▢	Antarctica
▢	Asia
▢	Australia
▢	Europe
▢	North America
▢	South America

South America's Land

The Andes Mountains are on the western edge of South America. These mountains form the world's longest mountain range. The Amazon River flows through South America. The world's largest tropical rain forest surrounds this river.

tropical
warm and wet

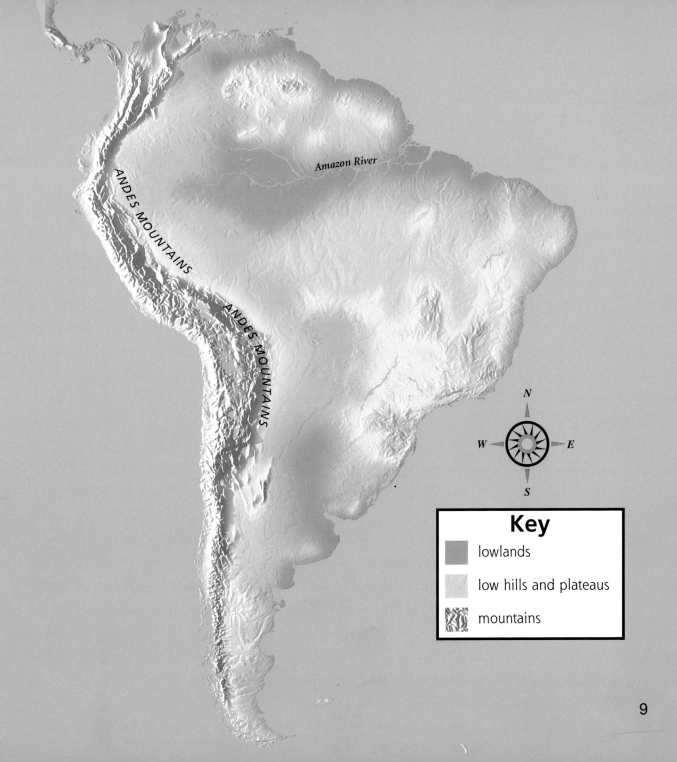

Amazon River

ANDES MOUNTAINS

ANDES MOUNTAINS

N

W   E

S

Key

lowlands

low hills and plateaus

mountains

9

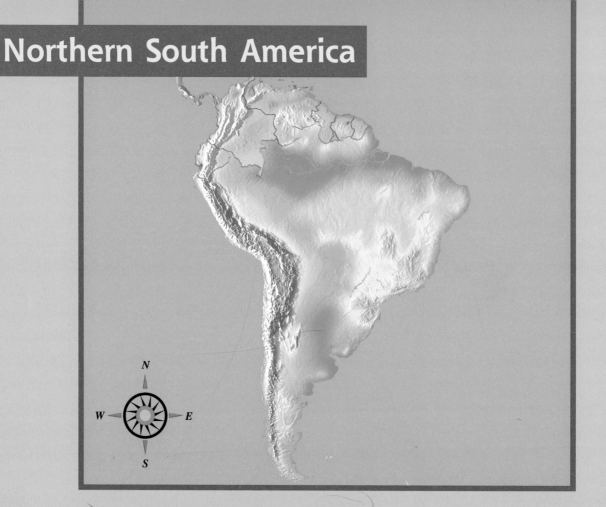

The soil in northern South America is good for growing crops. People grow coffee beans, cocoa beans, and bananas.

The northern region of South America also has many natural resources. Iron ore and oil are found in Venezuela.

region
a large area of land or water

11

Central South America

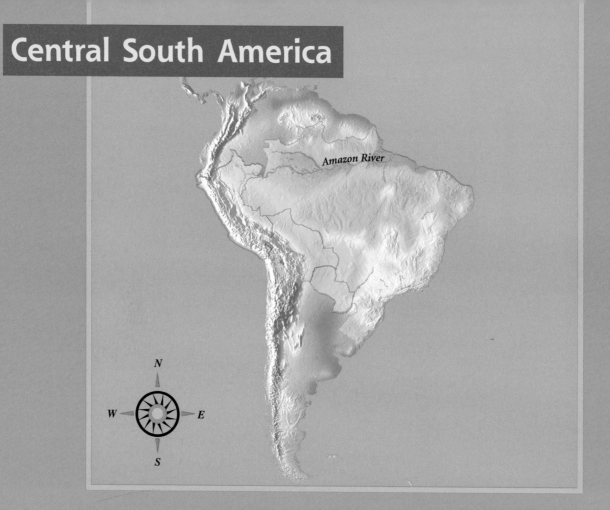

Amazon River

The Amazon River flows through central South America. Many plants and animals live in the Amazon rain forest.

People have cut down many of the rain forest's trees. They let their cattle graze on the land.

graze
to eat grass
and other plants

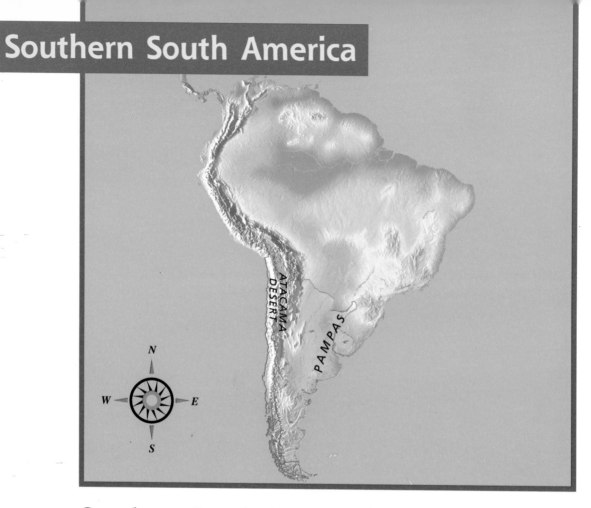

Southern South America

Southern South America has areas of grasslands, mountains, and deserts. Grasslands called the Pampas lie in Argentina and Uruguay.

Atacama Desert

Cattle and sheep graze on the Pampas. The Atacama Desert in Chile is the driest place on Earth. Rain almost never falls there.

Galápagos Islands

The Galápagos Islands lie west of Ecuador. Volcanoes created these 19 islands. People visit the Galápagos Islands to study the wildlife.

The islands' giant turtles weigh up to
600 pounds (272 kilograms). Iguanas, crabs,
and finches also live on the islands.

iguana
a large tropical lizard

South America's Animals

sloth

Many kinds of animals live in South America's rain forests and mountains. Sloths, tapirs, jaguars, and monkeys live in rain forests.

tapir

Many colorful birds nest in rain forest trees. Llamas and alpacas make their homes in the Andes Mountains.

alpaca

a camel-like animal that has long, silky wool used to make clothing

19

Most of South America's people live in cities. São Paulo, Brazil, is a large city on the east coast of South America.

People in Brazil speak Portuguese. People in most other South American countries speak Spanish.

Reading Maps: South America's Sights to See

1. Lake Titicaca in Peru is the world's highest lake. The lake is found 12,500 feet (3,810 meters) above sea level. Look at the map on page 5. If you were traveling from Colombia to Lake Titicaca, in which direction would you go?

2. Machu Picchu is an ancient city in the Andes Mountains. People called the Incas once lived there. Today, many people visit Machu Picchu. Is the Pacific Ocean to the east or west of Machu Picchu? Use the map on page 7 to answer this question.

3. Iguazú Falls is located along the border of Brazil and Argentina. You can see more than 275 separate waterfalls in this area. Look at the map on page 5. If you wanted to travel to Suriname from Iguazú Falls, in which direction would you go?

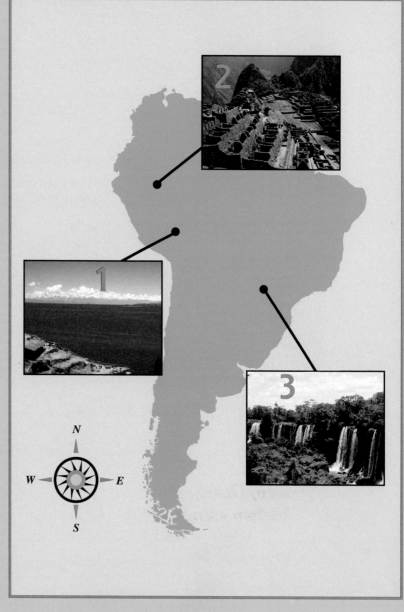

22

Words to Know

ancient (AYN-shunt)—from a long time ago

continent (KON-tuh-nuhnt)—one of the seven main landmasses of Earth

finch (FINCH)—a small songbird with a strong, thick bill used for opening seeds

llama (LAH-muh)—a large camel-like animal raised for its wool and used to carry loads

natural resource (NACH-ur-uhl REE-sorss)—a material found in nature that is useful to people

rain forest (RAYN FOR-ist)—a forest of tall trees that grows where the weather is warm and rainy all year

range (RAYNJ)—a chain or large group of mountains

sloth (SLOTH)—a mammal with long arms and legs; sloths move very slowly and hang upside down in trees.

tapir (TAY-pur)—a large, piglike animal that has hooves and a long nose

Read More

Fowler, Allan. *South America.* Rookie Read-about Geography. New York: Children's Press, 2001.

Petersen, David. *South America.* A True Book. New York: Children's Press, 1998.

Porter, Malcolm, and Keith Lye. *South America and Antarctica.* Continents in Close-Up. Austin, Texas: Raintree Steck-Vaughn, 2001.

Internet Sites

LatinWorld: South America
http://www.latinworld.com/sur
NationalGeographic.com—MapMachine
http://plasma.nationalgeographic.com/mapmachine/
  facts_fs.html
World Atlas Library of Maps
http://www.graphicmaps.com/aatlas/world.htm

Index